As you begin to pay attention to your own

stories and what they say about you, you

will enter into the exciting process of becoming,

as you should be, the author of your own

life, the creator of your own possibilities.

MANDY AFTEL

ACKNOWLEDGEMENTS

These quotations were gathered lovingly but unscientifically over several years and/or were contributed by many friends or acquaintances. Some arrived—and survived in our files—on scraps of paper and may therefore be imperfectly worded or attributed. To the authors, contributors and original sources, our thanks and, where appropriate, our apologies. –The Editors

WITH SPECIAL THANKS TO THE ENTIRE COMPENDIUM FAMILY.

CREDITS

Compiled by: Kobi Yamada

Designed by: Steve Potter

ISBN: 978-1-932319-33-0

CARE every day.

To the world you
may be just one
person, but to one
person you may
be the world.

JOSEPHINE BILLINGS

CARE every day.

When you care,
people notice.

SUSANE BERGER

CARE every day.

We must not only
give what we have,
we must also give
what we are.

CARDINAL MERCIER

CARE every day.

The effect of one
good-hearted person
is incalculable.

ÓSCAR ARIAS

CARE every day.

One by one, we
can be the better
world we wish for.

KOBI YAMADA

Every day do
something that will
inch you closer to
a better tomorrow.

DOUG FIREBAUGH

CARE every day.

I am seeking, I am
striving, I am in it
with all my heart.

VINCENT VAN GOGH

CARE every day.

I know what
pleasure is, for
I have done
good work.

ROBERT LOUIS STEVENSON

Do good and care
not to whom.

ITALIAN PROVERB

CARE every day.

The little things?
The little moments?
They aren't little.

JOHN KABAT-ZINN

CARE every day.

The place to
improve the world
is first in one's
own heart and
head and hands
and then work out-
ward from there.

ROBERT M. PIRSIG

CARE every day.

Care more than
others think wise.
Risk more than
others think safe.
Dream more than
others think practical.
Expect more than
others think possible.

UNKNOWN

CARE every day.

When you do
things from
the heart, it
usually works.

UNKNOWN

CARE every day.

To say yes, you
have to sweat and
roll up your sleeves
and plunge both
hands into life up
to the elbows.

JEAN ANOUILH

CARE every day.

The lure of
the distant and
the difficult is
deceptive. The
great opportunity
is where you are.

JOHN BURROUGHS

CARE every day.

Caring is
everything;
nothing matters
but caring.

FRIEDRICH VON HÜGEL

CARE every day.

Even when you
think your help
isn't wanted, it
usually is. Say it
again and again,
to everyone you
possibly can, "How
can I help you?"

DAN ZADRA

CARE every day.

No one has
ever become
poor by giving.

ANNE FRANK

CARE every day.

When you bring
a problem, bring
a solution.

SUSAN FIELDER

Don't make excuses—
make good.

ELBERT HUBBARD

CARE every day.

Love will find a
way. Indifference
will find an excuse.

UNKNOWN

CARE every day.

The people who
make a difference
are not the ones
with the credentials,
but the ones with
the concern.

MAX LUCADO

CARE every day.

Care is a verb.

CLARA BILLINGS

CARE every day.

A hero is someone
who has given
his or her life to
something bigger
than himself.

JOSEPH CAMPBELL

CARE every day.

There are those
whose lives affect
all others around
them. Quietly
touching one heart,
who in turn, touches
another. Reaching
out to ends further
than they would
ever know.

WILLIAM BRADFIELD

CARE every day.

You don't know
what you get back
until you give.

BILL CLAPP

CARE every day.

Don't just talk
about change,
or about helping
people. Make
it happen.

JOHN STANFORD

CARE every day.

Our deeds determine
us, as much as we
determine our deeds.

GEORGE ELIOT

CARE every day.

What is the city
but the people?

WILLIAM SHAKESPEARE

CARE every day.

We have to do the
best we can. This is
our sacred human
responsibility.

ALBERT EINSTEIN

CARE every day.

We can be wise
from goodness
and good
from wisdom.

MARIE VON EBNER-ESCHENBACH

CARE every day.

We each have
a choice: to
approach life as a
creator or a critic,
a lover or a hater,
a giver or a taker.

UNKNOWN

CARE every day.

Fill your life with
as many moments
and experiences
of joy and passion
as you humanly
can. Start with
one experience
and build on it.

MARCIA WEIDER

CARE every day.

What the heart
gives away is
never gone. It is
kept in the hearts
of others.

ROBIN ST. JOHN

I've learned
that just one
person saying
to me, "You've
made my day!"
makes my day.

ANDY ROONEY

CARE every day.

The work of your
heart, the work
of taking time
to listen, to help,
is also your gift
to the whole of
the world.

JACK KORNFIELD

CARE every day.

People who deal
with life generously
and large-heartedly
go on multiplying
relationships to
the end.

A.C. BENSON

CARE every day.

The thoughtful
little things you do
each day have an
accumulated effect
on all our tomorrows.

ALEXANDRA STODDARD

CARE every day.

Sometimes our light
goes out but is
blown into flame
by another human
being. Each of
us owes deepest
thanks to those
who have rekindled
this light.

ALBERT SCHWEITZER

CARE every day.

We must be the
change we wish to
see in the world.

MAHATMA GANDHI

CARE every day.

One must care
about a world
one will not see.

BERTRAND RUSSELL

CARE every day.

It is when we forget
ourselves that
we do things that
are most likely to
be remembered.

PARKER SWEETWATER

CARE every day.

No person was ever
honored for what he
received. Honor has
been the reward for
what he gave.

CALVIN COOLIDGE

CARE every day.

Nothing liberates
our greatness like
the desire to help,
the desire to serve.

MARIANNE WILLIAMSON

CARE every day.

All the darkness in
the world cannot
extinguish the light
of a single candle.

MARIA GAUTIER

CARE every day.

Sometimes if you
want to see a
change for the
better, you have
to take things into
your own hands.

CLINT EASTWOOD

CARE every day.

The dedicated life
is the life worth
living. You. must
give with your
whole heart.

ANNIE DILLARD

CARE every day.

Believe in
something big.
Your life is
worth a noble
motive.

WALTER ANDERSON

CARE every day.

Without involve-
ment, there is
no commitment.
Mark it down,
asterisk it, circle
it, underline it.
No involvement,
no commitment.

STEPHEN COVEY

CARE every day.

The quality of
our expectations
determines the
quality of
our action.

ANDRÉ GODIN

CARE every day.

Best now,
better later.

L.M. HEROUX

CARE every day.

What you are
will show in
what you do.

THOMAS A. EDISON

CARE every day.

Act well at the
moment, and you
have performed a
good action for
all eternity.

JOHANN KASPAR LAVATER

CARE every day.

Knowing that
we can make a
difference in this
world is a great
motivator. How can
we know this and
not be involved?

SUSAN JEFFERS

CARE every day.

There's nothing like
the feeling of sheer
joy of wanting to
get up and help the
world go around.

HEIDI WILLS

CARE every day.

Even if I can't cure,
I can still care.

SALLY KARIOTH, RN

CARE every day.

What you do is of
little significance;
but it is very
important that
you do it.

MAHATMA GANDHI

CARE every day.

True wealth is not
measured in money
or status or power.
It is measured
in the legacy we
leave behind for
those we love and
those we inspire.

CÉSAR E. CHÁVEZ

Caring is a very
powerful business
advantage.

SCOTT JOHNSON

CARE every day.

You are richer
today if you have
laughed, given,
comforted or
forgiven.

UNKNOWN

CARE every day.

Excellence is not
merely a skill.
It is an attitude.

RALPH MARSTON

A company should
stand for something,
fulfill a purpose, and
contribute something
useful—hopefully
something special,
even wonderful—or it
shouldn't bother being
a company at all.

DAN ZADRA

CARE every day.

One great, strong,
unselfish soul in
every community
could actually
redeem the world.

ELBERT HUBBARD

CARE every day.

The start to a
better world is
the belief that
it is possible.

UNKNOWN

CARE every day.

Every day we're
given small
opportunities to
bring someone
joy that can make
a huge difference
in a life.

DELILAH

CARE every day.

What we have
done for ourselves
alone dies with
us. What we have
done for others
and the world
remains and is
immortal.

ALBERT PIKE

CARE every day.

Our arms are long
enough to reach
for the tomorrow
we hope for.

LUCINDA JEFFERSON

Loving people live
in a loving world.
Hostile people live
in a hostile world.
Same world.

WAYNE DYER

CARE every day.

Let the beauty of
what you love be
what you do.

RUMI

CARE every day.

Each time you stand
up for an ideal you
send forth a tiny
ripple of hope.

ROBERT KENNEDY

CARE every day.

When we don't
enjoy what we do,
we only nick the
surface of our
potential.

DENNIS WHOLEY

CARE every day.

We are made to
reach beyond
our grasp.

OSWALD CHAMBERS

CARE every day.

One of the greatest
misconceptions
that people live in
is that they don't
make a difference.

MARTHA LOUIS

CARE every day.

I believe that we're
here to contribute
love to the planet—
each of us in our
own way.

BERNIE SIEGEL, M.D.

CARE every day.

You have the
power to make
someone's day.

DAN ZADRA

If you find it in
your heart to care
for somebody else,
you will have
succeeded.

MAYA ANGELOU

CARE every day.

Everything counts.
Everything helps
or hurts; every-
thing adds to or
takes away from
someone else.

STEVE GOODIER

The applause of
a single human
being is of great
consequence.

SAMUEL JOHNSON

CARE every day.

There is in each
of us so much
goodness that if
we could see its
glow, it would
light the world.

SAM FRIEND

CARE every day.

We rise by
lifting others.

ROBERT G. INGERSOLL

CARE every day.

The good you do
is not lost though
you forget it.

JIRI MASALA

CARE every day.

Bad things don't
happen because we
care, they happen
when we don't care.

ELIZABETH MATTHEWS

CARE every day.

We cannot hold a torch to light another's path without brightening our own.

BEN SWEETLAND

CARE every day.

The true riches
of life come from
the satisfaction of
knowing that your
life counted for
something, that you
gave back far more
than you took.

W. CLEMENT STONE

CARE every day.

If you are working
on something you
really care about,
you don't have to
be pushed—the
vision pulls you.

STEVE JOBS

CARE every day.

Blessed is the
influence of one
true, loving human
soul on another.

GEORGE ELIOT

CARE every day.

Too often we
underestimate the
power of a touch,
a smile, a kind word,
a listening ear, an
honest compliment,
or the smallest act
of caring, all of
which have the
potential to turn
a life around.

LEO BUSCAGLIA

CARE every day.

Some people
strengthen our
society just by
being the kind of
people they are.

JOHN W. GARDNER

CARE every day.

All we can ask
in our lives is that
perhaps we can
make a little
difference in
someone else's.

LILLIAN DAVIS

CARE every day.

Give all that you
have, in everything
you do. Help a
person at least
once a day. Never
expect anything
in return.

UNKNOWN

If love is truly a
verb, if help is a
verb, if forgiveness
is a verb, if
kindness is a verb,
then you can do
something about it.

BETTY EADIE

CARE every day.

...to look up and
not down, to look
forward and not
back, to look out
and not in and to
lend a hand.

EDWARD EVERETT HALE

CARE every day.

I could tell where
the lamplighter was
by the trail he left
behind him.

HARRY LAUDER

CARE every day.

Any activity
becomes creative
when the doer
cares about doing
it right, or better.

JOHN UPDIKE

CARE every day.

I believe you are
your work. Don't
trade the stuff of
your life—time—for
nothing more than
dollars. That's a
rotten bargain.

RITA MAE BROWN

CARE every day.

There is no
such thing in
anyone's life as an
unimportant day.

ALEXANDER WOOLLCOTT

CARE every day.

If you show people
you don't care,
they'll return the
favor. Show them
you care; they'll
reciprocate.

LEE G. BOLMAN & TERRENCE E. DEAL

CARE every day.

We are here to add
to the sum of human
goodness. To prove
the thing exists.

JOSEPHINE HART

CARE every day.

People may forget
what you said, and
people may forget
what you did, but
they will never
forget how you
made them feel.

UNKNOWN

CARE every day.

There is no better
way to thank God
for your sight than
by giving a helping
hand to someone
in the dark.

HELEN KELLER

CARE every day.

Without a sense
of caring, there
can be no sense
of community.

ANTHONY J. D'ANGELO

CARE every day.

You may be whatever
you resolve to be.
Determine to be
something in the
world and you will be
something. "I cannot"
never accomplished
anything. "I will try"
has worked wonders.

JOEL HAWES

We should seize
every opportunity to
give encouragement.
Encouragement is
oxygen to the soul.

GEORGE M. ADAMS

CARE every day.

Enthusiasm is the
most important
thing in life.

TENNESSEE WILLIAMS

CARE every day.

I have seen so
many good deeds—
people helped,
lives improved—
because someone
cared. Do what you
can to show you
care about other
people, and you
will make our world
a better place.

ROSALYN CARTER

CARE every day.

It's so hard when I
have to, and so easy
when I want to.

SONDRA ANICE BARNES

CARE every day.

Change yourself
and your work will
seem different.

NORMAN VINCENT PEALE

CARE every day.

You really can
change the world if
you care enough.

MARIAN WRIGHT EDELMAN

CARE every day.

The things that
matter the most in
this world, they
can never be held
in our hand.

GLORIA GAITHER

My hope still is
to leave the world
a bit better than
when I got here.

JIM HENSON

CARE every day.